Kickstart Your UX Career:
Get Ahead in UX and Product Design with Effective Stakeholder Communication

QUICK GUIDE: 1-2 HOURS

© Copyright Mike Newman, Sweet Spot Consulting 2024

For any UX or product designer, adaptation is key – it's not just about designing a product for the end-user but also shaping your process to fit within your working environment.

About the Author

Mike Newman is a User Experience and Product Design professional with over 20 years of experience. Recognised as an industry expert in User-Centred Design, he has helped numerous businesses enhance their digital products, making them more meaningful for users. Mike insists on a collaborative design process and a welcoming approach to mentoring other designers. His goal with this book is to help up-and-coming UX and product designers master the art of communicating design to stakeholders and co-workers, ultimately driving better user experience and product design outcomes and elevating their careers in design.

Preface

Kickstart Your UX Career is your essential guide to becoming a successful and influential UX and product designer by applying effective stakeholder communication skills.

It's written to assist design professionals, particularly those new to the field in User Experience, in transitioning from design implementers to strategic designers. It focuses on applying UX knowledge in real-world business settings and effectively dealing with stakeholders. It's a quick guide designed to rapidly upskill you in the art of communication for design, requiring just a couple of hours of your time as an audiobook or eBook.

A common challenge for designers, especially those starting out in their careers, is communicating to stakeholders, managers, and colleagues who may not be familiar with design, or have their own ideas and agendas about it. This book will help you navigate these real-world challenges, and gain leverage for your work.

Over the years, I have spoken to several successful UX professionals to understand how they communicate the value of their design work within their organisations. They shared many insights with me, including several common frustrations and challenges. Some of the common ones you may recognise are:

- An unwillingness to invest time and money in proper user research, including user testing
- Business requirement that dictate solutions instead of reflecting customer needs
- Misunderstandings about UX, such as confusing it with UI or visual design, or focusing solely on deliverables such as wireframes

What You'll Get from This Book

This book is for forward-thinking UX and product design professionals looking to improve their craft. My goal is to empower you to transition from a competent hands-on designer to an influential communicator with stakeholders. This requires strong communication and trust-building skills alongside your practical design skills.

You'll gain:

- Insights from other UX professionals on common problems and useful approaches
- Communication techniques to convey your UX message effectively
- Strategies to align colleagues and teams with your UX practice

Whether you're a designer at the start of your career seeking advice on dealing with stakeholders or an established professional looking to improve your soft skills, this book is for you.

Introduction

I've been a user experience professional with a design and usability background for 20 years, working across various industries including telecommunications, media, travel, finance and banking, government, construction, retail, and e-commerce. One of the main challenges I often faced in my early years as a designer was that the companies I worked for often didn't fully understand design or usability – or how to integrate it into their processes.

Early in my career, I worked in an internal design team for a large bank in England. This company was an early pioneer in user-centred design practices, utilising a usability process called Rapid Application Development (RAD). This technique used user research, low-fidelity prototyping, and usability testing to iterate product applications based on direct feedback from banking customers.

The hardest part of that particular role, I later realised, was not the design or usability work–that was fascinating and easy to learn–but dealing with various people and different personalities, including senior staff wanting to have their say despite clear evidence from users. This often left me frustrated and diverted me from doing my best work. I seemed to spend much of my time and energy not designing but learning to talk the lingo and trying to rationalise the design work, working more on "presenting design" rather than "doing design."

Mastering UX Communication

One key skill I have refined over the years, and a focus of this book, is the art of communicating design within organisations to stakeholders and decision-makers. From my experience and personal success as a designer, I'd say this skill is absolutely crucial for success as a UX designer or product designer.

One thing I've learned is that effective communication requires adapting to the unique quirks of an organisation and its culture. Every business is different, shaped by a group of unique human beings working together to achieve a specific goal. No matter the size of the organisation, its ecosystem consists of people with varying experiences, backgrounds, and agendas. Therefore, to be successful as a designer, it's essential to shape your process to fit within the organisation's environment, not just focus in on the design of a product or service for the end-user.

If you are starting out in UX or product design, navigating this business-human landscape can be challenging at first. Over the years, I have worked in many types of organisations, both client-side and in agencies, and have worked with, for, and managed other design professionals. A common pattern I noticed in all of these roles is that communicating design to stakeholders, managers, teams, and colleagues can often be more challenging than designing the product itself. If you're interested in design, hands-on skills are something you can easily learn, but mastering communication is not so easy and usually takes practice.

What is a Good User Experience?

As a UX or product designer, how many times have you heard a colleague or a stakeholder make a casual comment about UX like, "I don't think that is a good user experience," based purely on their subjective viewpoint?

In the early days, describing UX to others was simpler, but these days, it has evolved into a multi-disciplinary practice encompassing various terminology, including visual design, interface design, interaction design, information architecture, and usability. It overlaps with development, research, psychology, accessibility, content, and marketing. Moreover, it interlinks with other practices such as customer experience, service design, design thinking, and agile development. It's no wonder that UX designers often feel their work is misunderstood or that their organisation is misinformed about it.

In addition, UX and product design is no longer the sole responsibility of the designer. The overall experience of an end product is shaped by a team of people working together. Whether it's an app, a website, or something else, there are designers, developers, product owners, project managers, senior managers, stakeholders, and maybe clients, all contributing and influencing the end product.

Each perspective brings a different dialect. The language of a designer, developer, and business stakeholder is different. We may all use the same words, but often with different meanings. This can lead to confusion, frustration, and misinterpretation, which is why communication is a critically important skill in UX and product design.

Picking Your Battles

A while ago, at a UX design conference, I saw a presentation with a slide titled "Pick Your Battles," featuring a see-saw illustration.

One side of the see-saw was labeled "uselessly agreeable," and the other, "being a jerk no one can work with." This slide stuck in my mind because, in the real world, designers often face pressure to be "uselessly agreeable." This is where your employer might tell you to design something based on a personal preference or a requirement that's not based on proper user research. Following their direction without question means you are letting them predetermine what the user wants, which negates the true purpose of having UX expertise. But on the other end of the see-saw is the "argue till you're blue in the face" end. This is where your design ego might take over, and you become that person trying to dictate the design and demand that they're wrong and you're right - Constantly defending your design decisions.

Earlier in my career, I felt like I was on that see-saw, going up and down. There were days when I felt like I couldn't get my message through in the right way. I let decisions go that I didn't believe were good enough or found myself constantly demanding that I was right. In desperation, I started coming up with different strategies to back my arguments or convince others they were wrong, but still got nowhere. It was like I was speaking a completely different language.

Unfortunately, no qualification will teach you the soft skills needed to align your business communication with your users authentically and powerfully. But by using the techniques in this book, I hope you will gain more confidence in the practice of communicating design and ultimately build more trust and backing from your stakeholders.

Advocating Your Design

A key point to remember when starting out is that all UX and product designers need to learn how to evangelise their work within the organisation they work. Selling your process is an essential skill that can make a huge difference—not only in being able to do the work well and in the right way but also in providing clarity and understanding for others about how user experiences add value. This means not only listening to users and understanding their needs yourself but also presenting those user perspectives in a way that stakeholders can relate to and care about. The goal is to become the voice of the user, creating empathy for their needs, behaviours, and expectations among stakeholders and others in your team who have a direct influence on the design.

It's important to recognise, then, that user experience is not just about the user—it's also about the business. Every designer works within a business or for a business, and recognising that balance between users and the business is the key to creating successful outcomes. In fact, when you take a step back and look at it holistically, you can say that each UX designer has at least two types of user groups: those outside the organisation (your end-users) and those inside the organisation (your stakeholders and co-workers).

If you've read a few UX and product design books, you'll know that many of them focus on skills, processes, and methodologies around the application of designing. In this book, I will instead guide you on how to apply your skills more effectively within an organisation for maximum impact. My aim is to help you, the designer, better communicate the value of user experience within your organisation and find that balance between the user and the business to help build trust and respect for what you do.

Chapter 1: Own Your Hero's Journey

A few years ago, I discovered the concept of the "Hero's Journey." - The notion that popular culture frequently follows a hero's narrative of adventure and personal transformation. This struck me as also highly relevant to our careers as we all face professional obstacles that create struggles we need to overcome. In overcoming these struggles, we transform and become better versions of ourselves. This personal growth is part of our hero's journey, and we should embrace these challenges.

A few years back, during a series of life coaching sessions, I had a breakthrough while recounting a pivotal moment from my childhood that shaped my mindset towards my later career. During high school, I experienced what I now see as a defining moment in my hero's journey as a designer. I had produced some artwork that received top marks, as well as an award from the school. Nervous about accepting the award during morning assembly, I stood on stage in front of many students. Initially, I felt very proud of myself, but my feelings quickly changed when, instead of applause, I heard laughter and jeering from many of the faces looking back at me. My heart sank, and my stomach churned into knots. This moment, I now believe, had a lasting impact on me, leading me to prefer avoiding taking the spotlight and deflecting recognition, even into my adult life and professional career.

In my early days as a designer, I often avoided presentations and expressed my achievements through others' success, feeling more comfortable that way. I was happy to let others take credit for my contributions and I was very sensitive to feedback–a common trait for designers who make a career out of creating visual things and inviting subjective critique.

Eventually, I learned that what I was lacking in my early days were some basic skills and techniques to overcome the fear of presenting and managing critical feedback. I also needed the experience to understand the perspectives of stakeholders and other professionals, and simple communication techniques to create and showcase my work in a way that facilitated positive and constructive outcomes.

Mastering the right communication techniques is crucial for achieving the best results in UX and product design. Many UX design professionals, including myself, are deep-thinking problem solvers rather than extroverted communicators. Deep thinkers often need to switch from "think" mode to "talk" mode, so it can feel challenging when others put them on the spot, challenging their expert opinion.

While this "deep-thinking" mindset can feel challenging when it comes to presenting work and collaborating, it's actually the best trait to have as a UX or product designer. It means you are well-equipped to tackle complex problems and deliver thoughtful, user-centred designs. So, embrace your deep-thinking nature and enhance it with key communication skills that enable you to leverage it to the fullest.

Professional Challenges

Everyone's career journey is different, as every person faces their own unique challenges and hurdles to overcome. Here, I will share my friend's challenging path to becoming a senior UX designer.

She moved to Australia from Hong Kong, where she had worked for a 3D design agency. In Australia, she studied UX and UI design and, after graduating, got her first design job with a software start-up.

Adapting to working with Australian colleagues was very different from her previous experience. The first challenge was adjusting to the lifestyle and work social situations. She noticed many differences in the workplaces in Australia compared to back home, such as the casual 'chit chat,' which was different from what she was used to. For her, she realised that adapting to being a designer in Australia was not just about the work itself or learning a new language, but also about understanding the subtleties of communication and the differences in language itself. People often didn't realise how difficult it was for her to adapt. She felt uncomfortable with the 'chit chats' because her English wasn't as good as her colleagues'. It required a lot of effort to speak, and she didn't know what to say when engaged in more informal conversations.

At the start of her design career in Australia, she worked in more junior visual design roles, but her goal was to transition into UX design. To achieve this, she had to overcome several key communication challenges, as moving from visual design to UX design required much more collaboration with other teams. This was a massive hurdle for her and required intense communication, including interpreting business requirements, translating them into meaningful designs, and communicating back to stakeholders to gain buy-in.

One of the first things she shared about the challenges of being a designer was, "100% of your work gets presented and judged by managers," which made presentations daunting. The language barrier compounded this difficulty.

For her first few years as a UX designer, she had many anxieties to overcome. She felt self-conscious about her imperfect English. This often left her unclear about her responsibilities, and afraid to speak up. In fast-paced meetings, she was still processing information when it was time for discussion, as she needed to translate and process information in her head in Chinese before responding in English. She had to constantly think about her manner, tone, and the context of what she was saying. This cognitive process, combined with the language barrier, made her feel as though people didn't fully trust her experience, starting a vicious cycle. While her ability as a designer was excellent, she often felt stuck in a "junior team member" mentality, which affected her confidence.

Kickstarting a UX Career

When I met my friend, she had just joined our UX team. She excelled at the job as designer, gravitating towards work that required mostly hands-on design skills, rather than collaboration. Recognising her obvious ability, I made sure to listen to her ideas, provide suggestions, and encourage her to contribute to discussions.

She got involved in some workshops, broadening her horizon and sparking an interest in research and strategic design. Later on, as her confidence grew, she started a new job at a larger corporation where she worked with an expanded team of designers and managers.

Despite increased confidence, she still felt lacking in the ability to present work effectively. Shortly after, my friend decided to take a UX crash course, hoping it would help her build more confidence and increase her employability as a UX designer. The course covered theories, UX methodologies, and the principles of 'Research, Design, Test.' However, it didn't fully prepare her for the corporate world's real business problems and stakeholder engagement.

She shared with me the realisation that in the real world, you have to deal with real people and real challenges that are not necessarily covered in a UX course. You might present a concept, debate, discuss, and come up with a design solution. But then someone might say:

- "We can't do it because it's not feasible or viable."
- "My users wouldn't want that."
- "There's not enough time for user research."
- "You didn't test with enough users."

"There's no crash course to teach you how to overcome those real-world challenges," she said.

The UX course had helped her feel qualified, but it didn't address the communication skills and mindset needed for real-world application.

As she progressed through her career, she decided to take a big leap and moved again–this time to New York, where she worked for a fast-paced UX design agency, making presentations daily. While she recounts that this felt like doing it the hard way, it pushed her out of her comfort zone even more, rapidly honed her communication skills, and ultimately boosted her confidence as a UX designer.

When I asked my friend what career advice she would give her younger self, she shared the following insights:

- **Master the tools of the trade:** Good software skills won't help you communicate, but they give you the confidence to know you can always deliver.
- **Throw yourself in the deep end:** This forces you to learn and adapt quickly and build confidence through repetition.

- **Find a mentor:** Mentorship can be more valuable than any course and helps you become more comfortable talking about UX.

Mentoring in UX

Mentoring is really important. You can ask a senior manager to be your mentor, but a mentor can also be a friend or colleague. You could simply identify someone you trust and ask for advice. Many people, including myself, are always willing to share their knowledge and offer guidance, which is one of the reasons I have written this book.

Being a Mentor

Whatever stage you are in your career, it is also good to consider how you can mentor others. You don't have to wait for someone to ask you to be their mentor. Help those who want to learn what you do. Remember - a key trait of leadership is giving others the confidence they need to succeed.

Group Mentoring

Mentoring doesn't have to be face-to-face or just between two people. You can join one of many online UX community groups for advice and get ad hoc mentoring this way. The important thing to remember is that the relationships you have with others in the design community are critical in transitioning from a hands-on designer to a more strategic designer. You can't always do everything alone, whether it's getting a new job, learning a new process, or getting feedback on your work.

Chapter 2: Kickstarting Your Career as a UX or Product Designer

The journey I'm going to take you on is about transitioning from a process-driven UX design implementer to a strategic influencer in UX and product design.

As a UX or product designer, you'll need to balance the hard skills (the tools and methods) with the soft skills (communication, empathy, and understanding). Mastering UX tools and methods is essential to being able to deliver what you do and gives you confidence in your ability as a professional. However, becoming a strategic designer involves more than just technical skills. It requires the ability to communicate a UX vision, advocate for it, listen to feedback, and navigate conflicts effectively, among other things.

Mastering the Tools and Methods: As you progress in your career, you'll become proficient in various UX tools and methodologies. These form the foundation of your skillset and are essential for executing your design work effectively.

Building Strong Communication Skills: Effective communication is crucial in UX. You'll need to clearly articulate your ideas, present your work to stakeholders, and justify your design decisions in a way that avoids complaining or defending. Being able to convey complex concepts in an understandable and likeable way is a valuable skill.

Developing Empathy: Understanding the needs and pain points of users is at the core of UX design. Equally important is empathy towards your colleagues and stakeholders. Building strong relationships and being able to see things from others' perspectives will make you a more effective designer.

Listening to Feedback: Constructive feedback is essential in the design process. Learning to listen and act on feedback without taking it personally, while maintaining your vision, will help you grow as a designer.

Managing Conflict: In any collaborative environment, differences of opinion are inevitable. Developing the ability to manage disagreements professionally and find common ground while clearly getting your point across is essential for a harmonious work life.

By focusing on these areas, you can transition from a process-driven UX designer to a more strategic designer, gaining greater control over your career destiny.

Mastering Job Interviews for UX and Product Design

As a professional, you likely already have a resumé and a portfolio, and there are many examples and templates available online, so I'm not going to cover those. Instead, let's begin this communication journey with some simple but effective tips for job interviewing.

As a professional UX or product designer, mastering interviews is crucial. UX is fundamentally a communication role, and that communication often starts from day one when you engage with prospective employers for the first time. It's important to showcase your communication skills in action during your interview, and you are likely to be tested on certain key things. The good news is that one of the key tricks for any interview is being prepared and anticipating what others may ask you. In UX and product design, there are several patterns of questions that get asked frequently.

To get you started, here are some basic questions you may be asked. Keep them handy or fresh in your mind, and adapt the responses to fit your own interview style.

If your prospective employer is conducting a remote interview, consider having your answers written down on cards in front of you so you can quickly glance at them for a reminder when asked.

1. What's your background?

When a prospective employer asks you to tell them about yourself, it's important to describe yourself clearly and cover the breadth of what you can offer.

Example: "I am an end-to-end product designer. I am comfortable working with stakeholders, conducting discovery research, and user testing, all the way through to collaborating with UI designers and developers to deliver and test products. I describe myself as a problem solver at heart, passionate about Lean UX and Agile methodologies, and I always focus on delivering results."

2. What's your preferred UX process?

Have a couple of answers ready, such as Lean UX or Human-Centred Design (HCD). Be familiar with key aspects of these processes so you can describe and discuss them confidently. If it's a remote interview, have your process sketched out in front of you so you can refer to it if needed.

Memorising a UX conversation framework like PUGSIE or PUPSS can also help you discuss the fundamentals of UX systematically with stakeholders. These frameworks are super useful, and I'll provide more detail on them later.

3. Describe a challenge you've faced and how did you overcome it?

Think of realistic challenges with positive outcomes. Avoid discussing difficult people unless specifically asked. Focus on challenges like learning new skills, adapting to new environments, or using new software. Highlight your problem-solving skills, resilience, and ability to adapt. Most importantly, emphasise what you learned from the experience and how it has prepared you for future challenges.

4. Have you ever dealt with a difficult person at work? What did you do, how did you approach and overcome it?

This can be a daunting question, so keep your answer simple and honest. Explain how you took the time to understand others' motivations and bridged gaps through effective communication in a professional way.

For example, you might describe running a workshop to solve a disagreement with a co-worker. Describe how you sought to understand their perspective and found common ground through the co-design activity. Try to emphasise your ability to remain professional, respectful, and solution-focused, and end by highlighting the positive outcome of the situation and what you learned from the experience.

5. What drives or motivates you?

Examples: Design challenges, problem-solving, creativity, working with like-minded people, learning new things, adding value with your work and seeing results, especially with user feedback.

6. What is your proudest moment?

This doesn't have to be work-related, but it can be good to refer to a professional award or recognition, or a successful project you were part of. Be sure to highlight the team effort along with any successful outcomes.

7. What's a product or service you've seen recently that you really like?

This question is quite common but can catch you out if you're not prepared for it. It is designed to put you on the spot and test your awareness of design in the real world and how connected you are with the industry. Someone who can think of a good product or service experience demonstrates they have their finger on the pulse. So, always have a site, app, or other experience you can talk about. Explain what you liked about it, and avoid obvious choices like Apple or Spotify.

8. How do you keep up to date with UX trends?

You could say you engage actively with the design community, attend UX events, read industry blogs, and seek insights from more senior designers or mentors. Highlight specific resources or influential figures you follow, such as the Nielsen Norman Group, and ensure you are familiar with their work in case the interviewer wants to delve deeper. Mention your hands-on experience in the industry and how it contributes to your ongoing learning and adaptation to new trends.

9. What is your ideal environment?

You could say you work best in supportive, cross-functional teams where you can collaborate with other talented people in product design, such as POs, BAs, testers, developers, UI designers, and other UX or product designers. Emphasise the importance of harmony and adding value to the team.

10. How would a friend describe you?

Be sure to have a positive spin on whatever trait you choose.

Example: "My friends say I'm a good listener - this helps me a lot with user testing, where I find I enjoy and excel at understanding users' needs."

Example: "My partner says I'm impatient, but that's because I like to get on and get things done. However, I've learned that sometimes it's essential to step back and assess if more time is needed to address certain issues thoroughly."

Example: "People say I have a good sense of humour, so I enjoy working in a team that has a good vibe, but I'm also excellent at focusing and working hard."

11. What do you think is a significant trend shaping the future of design?

Have something prepared for this that shows you have your finger on the pulse. For example, you could talk about the increasing integration of AI and how that's impacting UX. Or you might mention something more pragmatic, like how design systems are evolving and becoming more sophisticated.

12. What is UX?

This might sound obvious, but many interviewers like to understand your perspective of what UX is, so be prepared for it and have a good answer! Here are some straightforward explanations provided by other experienced UX professionals:

UX is about...

- Designing the whole experience for the user of a product (e.g., a website or an app) to make it as easy to use and enjoyable as possible.
- The art of building simple and user-friendly products by empathising with the people who use them.

- Researching how users behave and what they need, then designing experiences for them on the web, in an app, or anywhere else they interact.
- Helping businesses transform ideas into products, ensuring the product improves people's lives while increasing business revenue.
- Designing apps and websites – the way they look and how you click and tap around them.

Questions to Ask Them

Usually an employer will ask if you have any questions for them, and it's good to always have a couple of thoughtful questions prepared. It's best to stick to simple, pragmatic questions that don't put the interviewers on the spot.

For example:

1. About the Job
What does a typical day look like?
What specific projects or tasks would I be focusing on?

2. About the Team
Can you tell me about the team I would be working with?
What is the team's process or structure?

3. About the Culture
What's it like to work there?
What do you or other UX designers like about it?

4. About Success
What would contribute most to success in this position?
What are the key skills or qualities you believe are essential for excelling in this role?

Avoid self-focused questions like "What's the salary?", "How many days off do I get?", and "Can I work from home on Fridays?" These are questions for later!

Record Your Common Questions

Take some time to craft strong responses to all the common questions you encounter. Write them down and be prepared for future interviews–whether they come in a week, a month, or years down the track. Interview questions will often follow trends, so it's helpful to keep notes and look for patterns.

Preparing for common questions and understanding how to present yourself can significantly enhance your confidence and effectiveness in interviews.

STAR Interview Method

The STAR method (Situation, Task, Action, Result) is a structured way of responding to behavioural-based interview questions. It's worth reading up on and preparing some responses in this format so you are familiar with it. Not all employers will follow this framework, but it's worth being prepared for it just in case.

Key Advice for all interviews

No Blaming, No Complaining, No Defending. This mindset will help you stay focused and positive during your interview.

Chapter 3: Taking Them on the Journey

Once you're in the door as a professional UX or product designer, it's time to start setting yourself up as a voice for your users. Being a UX advocate means not just designing great experiences but also selling the importance of user-centred design within your organisation.

We all understand the importance of UX, but conveying this to others can be challenging. Different roles within an organisation —such as senior managers or other team members, including developers, visual designers, project managers, and even other UX designers—may not immediately grasp its value.

I remember earlier in my career when I was more of a "design implementer." I had many preconceived ideas about what good design was, and having worked for an agency, I was trained to sell my design concepts to others as the expert knower of all things design.

When I first discovered usability testing, one of my designs was put in front of some real users, and I had an "ah-ha" moment where I suddenly realised my own biases as a designer. Just because I found something easy and obvious didn't mean others did. A business that's not familiar with user testing will always have its own biases too, where a stakeholder is convinced that something they've proposed is great, but when put in front of real users, it becomes obvious it's not so great.

User testing is not about highlighting flaws in other people's proposed ideas, though. I learned this the hard way when, earlier in my career, I naively pitched two different art directors' designs against each other in a user testing session because they couldn't decide which one to choose. This became a very sensitive battle of egos about who had designed it better. It was not a great outcome.

User testing should be about gaining insights to improve the design for users and ensuring it meets their needs, leaving all design egos at the door. Because of this, choosing the right moment to bring your co-workers and stakeholders along the journey to their own "ah-ha" moment is crucial. If done right, you will see them become advocates of user-centred design and back your work. If done wrong, you may get disagreeable comments despite your evidence, such as, "you didn't test with enough users."

To do this properly requires patience and an approach called "Taking them on the journey," where you gradually involve others in the process. This helps shift their focus from personal opinions to user needs. This not only improves the overall design but also fosters a collaborative environment where everyone is aligned with creating the best possible user experience.

Taking Your Stakeholders on the Journey

I like to think of UX as a blend of creativity and science. On the creative side, there's visual work like concepts, ideation, sketching, and storytelling. This involves generating innovative ideas, creating compelling visuals, and designing intuitive interfaces that engage users. On the scientific side, there's psychology, testing methods, data collection, and analysis. This involves understanding user behaviour, conducting usability tests, gathering quantitative and qualitative data, and analysing findings to inform design decisions. UX design spans this spectrum, and as a UX designer, you will encounter people with varying levels of understanding about where UX sits on that spectrum.

Some might see UX as primarily related to "how it looks and feels" rather than "what it does" or "how it works." Others may associate UX design more with information architecture or purely as a role for delivering detailed wireframe specifications to developers. In reality, UX and product design as a practice can and should encompass all these aspects and more, especially where they contribute to a better end-user experience.

A designer's role includes educating and evangelising their user experience process within the business. Success in this endeavour isn't just about talking though; it's about demonstrating UX in action and letting others experience it. Collaboration is crucial, involving relevant parties in your process to help them understand and promote good UX themselves.

In my career, I transitioned from being a "design implementer" - trying to solve all design problems myself - to a "design facilitator" - solving design problems as a team. As the design implementer, I was expected to have all the answers, which was challenging. As the design facilitator I foster collaboration and initiate co-design workshops, which, although difficult at first, lead to much better outcomes. Being a design facilitator is more effective and less prone to failure because everyone has the opportunity to contribute and feel heard. Additionally, it allows you to get inside the heads of people in your immediate ecosystem and identify potential issues or design risks so you can address them much earlier, avoiding last-minute defending of your committed designs.

These days, most people understand the value of co-design - it's kind of *"the thing."* However, being a design facilitator and running workshops isn't easy. You still have to navigate different personalities and sometimes face resistance or disinterest. You may be asked to involve certain people, such as a senior manager, who might attend expecting you to have all the answers. They might bring their own ideas and not want them challenged, try to dominate just to be seen as the leader in the room, or simply see workshops as a waste of their time and decline to attend at all. Despite these challenges, facilitating collaborative design sessions is key to effectively advocating for UX within your organisation.

By effectively communicating the value of UX through co-designing, you can help your organisation see the benefits of a thorough approach, ultimately leading to better user experiences and more successful projects.

Understanding Who You Are Talking To

One of the many challenges designers face is when the business doesn't fully understand UX or how to integrate it effectively into their existing processes. UX and product design are very specialised professions with their own acronyms and methodologies, so it's not surprising that they are sometimes misunderstood. As designers, when we interact with our users, we usually tailor our words and questions to their persona, avoiding jargon and industry terminology, but in a business environment, we often don't.

In a world where everyone can master the hands-on design tools, and with AI helping to accelerate the day-to-day stuff, becoming a modern UX designer is more about being a great communicator within your organisation–and that means being sensitive to your organisation's way of speaking, as well as your users'.

Start by acknowledging that your organisation's language is different from yours, and to be successful, you need to empathise with your co-workers as well as your users, and be their translator for UX jargon and terminology.

Understanding Your Stakeholders

Getting to know your users also means getting to know your stakeholders. This will help you understand where decision-makers are coming from. Establishing a connection with your stakeholders builds trust and credibility and provides an opportunity to explain what you do and how you can work together. Use insights from discussions and meetings to bring extra value to your team.

Stakeholder Interviews

A stakeholder interview can be one of the most effective ways to kick off a new job or project. It helps you understand what stakeholders really want and allows you to get inside their heads. There are many free templates available online to get you started if you want to do this in a structured way. However, you can instead just organise a catch-up over coffee, a one-on-one meeting, a call, or even a casual chat in the corridor. Your key aim is to learn more about the business needs and continually cross-pollinate your world with theirs.

Understanding Your Co-Workers

Having empathy for your co-workers is crucial. Understanding their needs and pain points allows you to communicate more effectively and work more collaboratively. One excellent method to gain this understanding is to create team personas. Similar to user personas, these are focused on the needs and motivations of your co-workers and stakeholders.

By understanding the goals and priorities of key team members, such as your product owner or developer, you can better align your efforts. For example, if a product owner is particularly sensitive to timelines and focused on delivering product increments as quickly as possible, knowing this can help you tailor your communication and work process to better align with their motivations.

You don't need to go overboard with these personas–treat them as proto-personas. You don't need to share them with anyone unless you find it beneficial. It's the process of creating them that's important. Whether on a piece of paper, a whiteboard, or more formally as a design artefact, doing this exercise will help you shift into the mindset of a design facilitator rather than a design implementer.

There are also plenty of existing resources and ideas out there to guide you in creating team personas, so take action now to research and develop ones that are relevant to your team structure. This effort will certainly enhance your ability to collaborate and communicate effectively within your team.

Speaking the Same Language

Having some team personas leads onto the next part - being able to speak the same language. Properly understanding your co-workers' priorities and goals is crucial for how to explain UX to them in ways that are clear and easy to understand. This is similar to how you tailor your language when talking to users.

With developers, rather than just handing them something to implement, involve them in the design process. This helps them understand the methodology and data behind your decisions, leading to a shared understanding of each other's goals and allowing them to feel heard and valued as key contributors to the user experience. It helps them see the benefits of their work directly when real users provide positive feedback. Remember, understanding their needs and pain points is important, so you can learn to communicate in ways that resonate with them.

For example -

Developers may be sensitive to having to recode work. Their focus might be on delivering code quickly and accurately, so it can be frustrating for them to revisit their work. They may feel more comfortable having everything delivered upfront, all nicely specced out, so they can get in the zone and focus for a few hours. When communicating with developers, you might frame collaborative UX activities in terms of driving more accurate designs, which result in less rework in the long run.

When communicating with project managers, you might highlight how UX provides an opportunity to validate designs early to catch unforeseen problems.

With executives, you might focus on describing UX in terms of ROI and customer loyalty.

Building Trust Through Empathy

In UX, user empathy is crucial. The same applies to your interactions with colleagues and stakeholders. Approach every interaction with the mindset of understanding their perspectives and motivations, which not only leads to stronger relationships but also helps build trust. Be clear, concise, and transparent in your interactions.

By focusing on understanding and empathising with your co-workers and stakeholders, you will be better placed to start building a collaborative environment where UX is valued and integrated into business processes, allowing individual voices to be shared and heard. This not only helps in delivering better user experiences but also in establishing your credibility and advancing your career in UX through alignment and trust.

Chapter 4: Communicating UX to Non-UX People

Explaining what you do as a UX or product designer can be challenging. People often misunderstand UX, sometimes attaching it to other more familiar terms like web design, IT, or customer service. This chapter will provide straightforward strategies for explaining UX to others, why it matters, and how to start getting them onboard with your process using a simple collaboration activity.

Communicating UX to Your Immediate Team

Each business and team member has a different level of understanding of UX. Some teams may be quite mature but resistant to new viewpoints, while others may have a very basic understanding, requiring you to start from scratch. The key is to communicate consistently and involve your team in the UX process wherever possible, adapting your approach to meet their specific needs and fostering a culture of continuous learning and collaboration.

Speaking in Layman's Terms

It may seem obvious, but when speaking to those who are less familiar with UX, describe it in simple terms that are clear and easy to understand without being patronising.

For instance, you could clarify the difference between UX and UI by showing a slide in one of your presentations that explains how UX and UI fit into the overall process. Highlight that UI is a component that helps make the user experience better but is not, in and of itself, the entire user experience. There are some great illustrations on the web that help explain this, including one that I've used many times and works well with stakeholders.

The illustration shows a user and a bicycle as a product. The handlebars, seat, and pedals of the bike are labeled as the "UI," while an image of the user riding the bike and having a great experience is labeled as "UX."

Ultimately, I find it beneficial to use this example when framing UX as a toolkit of methods and approaches designed to improve user experiences. By showing the difference between UI and UX, I can better explain why UX is not just a deliverable like a user interface design.

Gradually Involve Your Team

Take your team on the journey by involving them in the UX process. Use "What is UX?" presentations with key slides like the above bicycle example to demonstrate your process and how it works within your organisation. This could be a dedicated presentation focusing on your entire approach, but it can also be done more iteratively by integrating key slides into existing design presentations to reinforce the value of UX over time.

Once your immediate team starts to show understanding towards your perspective, start spreading the message more outward to stakeholders and key decision-makers. You could ask to do a 'UX Roadshow', scheduling a series of presentations to key personnel about what UX means to the organisation, how it relates to them, and how they can get more information.

Socialise Your Work

Look for ways to promote your UX work for visibility and extra credibility. Use office wall space or create a Wiki page to help communicate what you do. Showcasing your work helps others understand the value of UX and invites their input.

UX Design Principles Workshop

You can enhance the rationale behind your process by grounding it in solid UX principles. Where possible, conduct dedicated workshops that include decision-makers to establish these principles, ensuring their buy-in.

A UX principles workshop helps align team members and stakeholders with the user's perspective, fostering a shared understanding of the importance of a robust user experience process.

There are many ways to run these workshops, so I won't delve into them in this book. To get started, you can search online for a simple format that suits your needs. As with all workshops, begin small and gradually build up–initially involving your immediate team. Then, when comfortable, start bringing in key decision-makers for their input and approval. Don't skip this last step, as it is crucial for achieving buy-in and validating your UX principles.

'Rule of Thumb' Principles

Another approach is to start simply by introducing and aligning your team around established usability principles like Jakob Nielsen's 10 Usability Heuristics for User Interface Design or showcasing other UX design principles from industry leaders like Google, Apple, Uber, and Spotify, which provides credibility. Then, you can workshop your own UX principles to replace or supplement those. This approach can help create a shared foundation for your principles.

In Summary

Communicating UX effectively requires clear, consistent messaging tailored to your audience's understanding and needs. By involving your team early and facilitating collaborative design, you can bridge the gap between UX and non-UX stakeholders.

Chapter 5: Navigating Common UX Challenges with Stakeholders

This chapter delves into some communication challenges you may face as a beginner in UX and some key approaches on how to address them effectively, as used by other professional UX designers. It's about equipping you with the tools to handle issues as they arise, ensuring you can move from understanding the principles to doing the practical, real-world work.

Common UX Challenges

Navigating a stakeholders ignorance or dismissal of UX is a common obstacle for many UX designers. To transition from being 'doers' who deliver designs and wireframes to 'strategic thinkers' who occupy lead and senior roles, understanding and addressing the common challenges is crucial.

This chapter will help you address key challenges by highlighting common approaches used by experienced UX and product designers to effectively communicate the importance of the "User" in User Experience.

UX Challenge:
Stakeholder Bias and Misconceptions

UX and product designers can often encounter resistance from stakeholders who believe they already understand what users want. These stakeholders, being experts in their field, may be wrapped up in their own ideas and feel they are very familiar with their users' issues already. This can sometimes lead to dismissive comments about user feedback, such as, "I already knew that," or, "I don't think our users will want to do that," or simply, "I disagree".

Stakeholders might also use UX terminology casually and without substance, making statements like, "Doing this (their idea) will create a better user experience," "If I were a user, I would want (their idea)," or "That (someone else's proposed idea) is a bad user experience."

Approach:

Get inside their heads

Set up 'stakeholder safaris': Organise groups of stakeholder interviews to understand their perspectives and uncover any preconceived notions about users.

Use these interviews to establish a connection with your stakeholders. This helps them see you as a partner in achieving the business goals rather than an outsider challenging their ideas.

Develop personas for your stakeholders: Take the time to really understand their needs, motivations, and pain points. This will help you tailor your communication and collaboration efforts more effectively.

By understanding your decision makers better, you can adapt your way of working and start to use terminology that resonates with them. When stakeholders feel understood, they are more likely to be open to UX insights.

Approach:

Involve Them in Your Process

Demonstrate the value: All user experiences are measurable. Find ways to show how your UX process leads to better outcomes. When stakeholders witness the benefits of involving users in the design process, they are more likely to support UX efforts.

Invite them to user testing and design workshops: Let stakeholders see firsthand the data and insights gathered from real users. This can help them understand the importance of user-centred design.

Present case studies and real-world examples: Highlight successful projects where UX research and testing, for example, has led to positive results.

Regular updates: Keep stakeholders informed about UX activities and progress. Use clear, concise, and relatable language and continue to reinforce the importance of UX over time.

Approach:

Pro-Actively Address Misconceptions

Clarify what UX is and isn't: Take opportunities in conversation to educate stakeholders about the full scope of your UX process. Emphasise that UX goes beyond visual design or delivering wireframes – it is a practice that spans research, testing, and iterative improvements.

Counter dismissive comments: When stakeholders make casual remarks about UX, provide evidence-based responses. For instance, if someone says, "I already knew that," respond with, "That's great! We've been able to validate it for you with user feedback."

If someone says, "You didn't test with enough users," you could respond with, "I know it seems like a low number, but research shows that for usability testing, five users is optimal. After that number, you get diminishing returns for the time and money spent." You can refer them to an article about it, such as one from the Nielsen Norman Group.

Alternatively, you could say, "What number did you have in mind?" or "This was a qualitative piece, but you're right, it would be good to back it up with some quantitative research too."

Frame UX in business terms: Translate user feedback into actionable insights that align with business objectives. For example, instead of just saying, "Users found this feature confusing," also mention the benefits of taking action, "Improving this feature will reduce user errors and increase efficiency, leading to higher user satisfaction and potentially increased engagement."

UX Challenge:
Budget and Time Constraints

UX may be seen as a roadblock rather than a time and cost saver. Stakeholders might view UX as an unnecessary expense, opting to trim it back in the project timeline or try to squeeze out deliverables too late in the process.

MVP misconceptions

MVP, or Minimum Viable Product, is a term used frequently in agile methodology to denote the smallest increment of a product with enough features to validate a product idea and gather user feedback. The purpose of an MVP may be misunderstood by some stakeholders, leading to a "build it now and change it later" mentality–disregarding the importance of user validation in favour of releasing it quickly and deferring any problems or risks until later.

Approach:

Always test 'something'

Utilise guerrilla testing or corridor testing to conduct user research within limited time or budgets. Start by proving something small and build upon their appetite for it incrementally. Remember–you can always do something, even if it's just a bit of desk research. Be disciplined in ensuring that users always have a place in the process.

Approach:

Evangelise Your Process

Reinforce that UX is an ongoing practice that spans an entire project lifecycle, not just a deliverable. Emphasise the importance of planning UX activities at the start, middle, and end for successful project outcomes.

UX Challenge:
The HiPPO (Highest Paid Person's Opinion)

Stakeholders may favour their own ideas over your solutions, even if you back them with solid user research. Outcomes, therefore, may end up being based on seniority rather than actual user needs, leading to non-customer-centric decision-making.

Approach:

Influence, Don't Argue

Often, you'll find you can't argue with a HiPPO when they are invested in their own idea, but you can influence their decision-making process over time. Developing your communication skills to influence rather than defend your design decisions is crucial.

Here are some ways to start being an influencer:

Validate assumptions: Emphasise that ideas and business requirements are just assumptions that need validation through UX research. For example, say, "While this idea sounds promising, let's test it with users to see if it truly meets their needs."

Showcase the ROI: Present case studies and data demonstrating the return on investment for investing in proper design validation. For instance, you might show how a previous project led to increased user engagement or sales due to user-centred design improvements.

Get Them Excited: Experiment to identify what excites your stakeholders. Maybe it is data, customer videos, or industry trends. Use these elements to engage them and get them thinking about ideas that involve users instead.

For example:

- Share compelling statistics that highlight the importance of UX, such as, "Companies that invest in UX see a 37% increase in revenue."
- Show clips of user testing sessions to bring to life real user experiences and feedback*
- Highlight current trends and best practices in UX to demonstrate how a user-centered approach aligns with industry standards, referencing well-known exemplary UX brands like Google, Apple, or Spotify.

By adopting some of these approaches, you can gradually shift the focus from individual opinions to evidence-based ideas, fostering a more user-focused approach within your organisation.

*Remember to ensure compliance with privacy regulations when sharing user videos, including obtaining user consent and masking or de-identifying users when necessary to protect their privacy within your organisation.

Chapter 6: Finding the Sweet Spot Between the User and the Business

Finding a sweet spot between users and business needs is crucial because every organisation you work in requires a balance of both. Without a business need, you would not have a job. This balance ensures that the products and services you design are not only user-friendly but also align with the business goals, creating value for both the users and the organisation.

One critical aspect of effectively navigating challenges in UX is recognising the common signals that indicate potential issues in the design process. These signals are indicators of a misalignment between the user and business needs. By being aware of these signals, you can proactively address them and ensure that your design decisions remain user-focused.

Watch Out for These Common Signals

- **Stakeholders Making Decisions on Behalf of Users**: Stakeholders might state they already know what makes a good user experience, leading to decisions that don't truly reflect user needs.

- **UX Presentations Focused on Personal Preferences**: Discussions often get sidetracked into subjective likes and dislikes, rather than objective user needs.

- **Assumptions Used as Business Requirements**: Assumptions are treated as *requirements* and lack proper user input, leading to features that don't solve real user problems.

- **UX is Seen as a Deliverable, Not a Process:** Stakeholders ask you to "do the UX" for a page or feature, when they actually mean a UI design or a wireframe, overlooking the iterative process and any user research necessary.

Let's look at some strategies and techniques you can use to start bridging the gap between the UX world and the world of stakeholders and co-workers. These strategies will enhance your ability to communicate effectively and build stronger support for your work over time.

Highlight Common Misconceptions

It's essential for designers to consistently articulate what UX is in a way that is easy to understand and should be frequently reiterated. The term 'design' can often mislead clients and stakeholders into thinking UX is just about the 'look and feel.' Therefore, it's crucial to explain and reiterate that UX is a *practice*, not a *deliverable*. It encompasses the entire user experience, including research, testing, and iterative improvements over time.

Fit the Audience

Adapt your communication style to your audience. Instead of using UX terminology and jargon, focus on speaking the same language as the business. When presenting to senior executives, use high-level summaries and emphasise business outcomes like increased customer satisfaction.

Sometimes, it can be beneficial to also shift your language from 'user testing,' which may seem too involved, to terms like 'quick validation' or 'sense check' with users to make it more palatable for stakeholders.

Become Your Users

Act as the voice of the user in meetings and workshops. Know your persona groups inside out and represent their perspectives in discussions.

Leverage Your Design Skills

Visual aids can be powerful tools in your arsenal. Kick off briefs with a whiteboard session, allowing you to visually map out ideas and encourage collaborative input. Sketch journey maps to illustrate user experiences clearly and concisely. For remote work, use collaborative tools like Miro or Figma (FigJam) to maintain engagement and ensure everyone is on the same page. By using these visual methods, you can simplify complex ideas and make your points more compelling and accessible, playing to your strengths as a designer.

Build Alliances

Start by gaining buy-in from your own UX team and other supportive team members. Once you have their backing, venture outwards to build alliances with other departments. Having a strong internal network can help amplify your message and provide additional support when advocating for UX initiatives.

A good way to do this is to design collaboratively with your team, and use peer reviews and dry-runs to test your presentations. Peer reviews involve team members reviewing each other's work to catch errors and offer feedback, while dry-runs are practice presentations to refine your delivery before presenting to stakeholders.

Practice Co-Design Frequently

This approach allows co-workers and stakeholders to provide input and become advocates for UX within the organisation.

Collaborative design is beneficial because you can later say, "This is what we designed together." This differs from presenting your designs and asking for critique, which can be polarising and encourage subjective debate. Maintaining collaboration throughout the project helps avoid surprises and keeps everyone invested in the outcome.

Here's how to start with Co-Designing:

Start Small and Build Up

Start by running small workshops to learn and refine the process. Conduct a proposal workshop or a design briefing session on a whiteboard with another designer for 15 minutes. Gradually add a non-designer and build from there until you can confidently include a key stakeholder.

Running a bigger workshop can present challenges, such as late arrivals or dealing with difficult personalities like a loud senior manager playing Devil's Advocate or a Doubting Thomas picking apart every detail. Build up to it at your own pace if you can, but don't be deterred; the benefits far outweigh the challenges.

Understand Your Audience

Collaboration techniques involve working together and ensuring individual voices are shared and heard, so always consider your communication strategy to include everyone in the room. Before presenting anything, it helps to fully understand your audience. Have clear goals and practice your presentation or workshop with peers for a sense-check on its suitability as well as another chance to collaborate.

Navigating Remote and Hybrid Collaboration

Working remotely and dealing with international teams has become more frequent. Fortunately, with the rise of online whiteboarding tools, the old days of pointing a camera at a physical whiteboard are long gone. Tools like Miro, MURAL, and Microsoft Whiteboard have been commonplace for a while now, making remote workshops seamless and interactive.

While remote workshops are crucial, never underestimate the power of in-person collaboration. Many companies are now opting for hybrid teams with designated office days. These office days are excellent opportunities to bring people together who often work from home. On these days, people are usually more engaged and eager to interact with others, making it an ideal time for collaborative sessions.

Co-Create Your User Personas

Creating personas as a group is a fantastic way to kick off a new project and foster team collaboration.

When your co-workers are involved in creating personas, they become more invested in the user outcomes. This collaboration ensures they understand and empathise with your users, making it easier to refer to these personas confidently. As a result, your co-workers are more likely to support you in user-focused discussions when needed.

There are various approaches to creating personas, but here's a common process outlined:

- **Qualitative Personas Workshop:** Start by gathering insights from initial user interviews. Then, workshop some ideas with co-workers and stakeholders to create a proto-persona (a rough outline). This step is your 'draft'—a bunch of assumptions that don't prove anything yet. Stick them up on the wall or place them prominently in a shared drive or team page. Emphasise that they are iterative and should be updated as you gather more data.

- **Quantitative Validation:** After creating your proto-personas, you can start conducting surveys and analytics studies, such as examining site traffic data, user behaviour metrics, or other relevant statistics. This step involves validating your qualitative findings with quantitative data, refining your proto-personas into more accurate and reliable user personas as you gain more insights.

Risks and ROI

When speaking to executives, use language they relate to, such as risk management and Return On Investment (ROI). Here are some examples of conversation techniques:

Without effective customer feedback, we can't build it properly

Example - "We can proceed without user testing, but unless we are sure about x, we may end up having to re-do it later, costing extra time and money."

Example - "This is our best guess based on what we know today, but x is still unanswered. Do you want us to investigate further or proceed without?"

Example - "Your budget is $x. Surely you can invest in some user testing? It's a small amount of the overall cost and will ensure you deliver the intended results."

The Evidence

Using real data to support your UX recommendations is invaluable. Data analytics, heatmaps, and other visual analytics tools can help you present solid evidence.

Don't Sweat the Small Stuff

Focus on what you see as the important issues and avoid testing every minor detail to prevent resistance from the team. Use corridor tests for quick data and invest in more rigorous user testing when necessary.

The Measured Value of UX

Metrics are important to prove that UX adds value to the bottom line. Use frameworks like SEQ, SUS, SUPR-Q, and Google Heart to measure and communicate the impact of your work. If you can, start to create a UX dashboard to reinforce success metrics, customer feedback, and any supporting research and how it's improving over time.

First-hand Experience

Involving stakeholders in the UX process at every step is key. This can begin with interviewing them as Subject Matter Experts (SMEs) in their area of expertise, inviting them to observe customer interviews, and having them participate in co-design workshops.

The "Ah-ha" Moment

Presenting user evidence is crucial for building empathy and understanding. Conduct frequent user interviews, using guerrilla testing if necessary, to gather insights that highlight the value of UX. Share user data and, if possible, real video feedback* with stakeholders. Seeing feedback firsthand fosters empathy and encourages them to generate more user-centred ideas based on the problems they have personally witnessed, rather than their own ideas.

Again, remember to ensure compliance with privacy regulations when sharing user videos, including obtaining user consent and masking or de-identifying users when necessary to protect their privacy within your organisation.

The FOMO (Fear Of Missing Out) Effect

Some stakeholders are highly motivated by the actions and successes of other companies and strive to be perceived as being aligned with industry leaders. Sharing industry case studies of high-profile companies like Google, Apple, and Spotify can inspire and motivate stakeholders. Additionally, conducting a competitive analysis can highlight gaps in their current approach and drive stakeholders to invest more in your process. This approach not only helps them avoid being outperformed by competitors but also provides exciting reference points that they can use in their own presentations.

A Change of Mindset

Changing the mindset of your stakeholders and colleagues is one thing, but you also need to ensure your own mindset is in alignment with the business you work for. It's not just about convincing others to do more user-centred design; it's about building empathy, fostering understanding, and creating a shared vision of what good UX can achieve together.

Moreover, it's crucial to align UX goals with business objectives. Show how UX improvements can lead to increased customer satisfaction, reduced costs, or higher revenues. Use language and metrics that resonate with your audience. Remember, you're not just advocating for good design; you're advocating for better business outcomes.

Chapter 7: Tools for Effective Conversations with Stakeholders and Decision Makers

Mastering the process of design communication within a business is not just an art form—it's also about having the right tools and know-how to conduct yourself appropriately. UX is a very crowded space, and designers who possess the business acumen to conduct themselves in the real world of business will more easily stand out. Employers seek UX designers who have not only software skills, user research expertise, and a proven design eye but also the capability to communicate and present their work effectively to stakeholders.

The difference between being a good communicator and a great communicator in UX lies in understanding how to get your point across effectively and solve problems or defuse debates. For this, you can learn and use a conversation framework to guide you.

The T.E.S.L.A. Principles for Effective UX Communication

Effective communication is at the heart of successful UX design. The T.E.S.L.A. principles were created to help articulate all the important aspects of great communication in design. These principles break down the key components that UX designers need to master to engage stakeholders, align team members, and ensure their designs have a meaningful impact.

T is for Talking

This is the most obvious skill when considering how to communicate effectively. To be a successful UX designer and gain more leverage for your practice, your choice of words is crucial. Adopt a style of language that your business can relate to. You need to clearly articulate the problem you are trying to solve, the outcomes you want to achieve, and the process you intend to adopt to achieve it in a way your clients or stakeholders understand and care about.

The other aspect of talking is combining what you say with how you say it. Using the right tone of voice to influence people and learning how to put them at ease is very helpful. When you can put others at ease, it also puts you at ease.

E is for Expression

Expression, also known as body language, is a key aspect of communication. When observing user behaviour, you pay close attention to what users do, as well as what they say, and it's the same for you when dealing with stakeholders and co-workers. Practicing positive body language gives you confidence, which is conveyed to whomever you are communicating with. This will make you feel better and more confident in how you respond to others.

S is for Sketching

Designers are good at communicating in pictures, so tapping into your visualisation skills as often as you can to articulate your points to stakeholders and co-workers is very effective. While a good designer can do good design, an excellent designer can also facilitate good design amongst a group of others. Learning the art of facilitating design workshops is crucial for design leadership roles and this includes knowing when to kick off a whiteboard session or remote workshop to solve a problem or defuse a debate.

L is for Listening

Being a good communicator is not just about having the gift of the gab. A critical characteristic of a good communicator in UX is being a good listener. You already know that you can't fully understand your users' needs or preferences if you don't listen to what they tell you. The same applies to your organisation—how can you understand your business needs if you are preoccupied with your own view? Learning to really listen and understand your stakeholders will increase your trust and credibility, enabling you to do more UX work and add more value to the lives of your users.

A is for Adaptation

An important aspect of UX communication is being able to adapt to fit the individual quirks of an organisation and its culture. Every business is different, determined by a group of unique human beings working together to achieve a specific goal. Adaptation as a UX designer is key to navigating the varying experiences, cultural backgrounds, personal and career agendas, and different personalities within any organisation.

Conversation Frameworks

Earlier, we explored common communication strategies for addressing UX challenges. Now, let's delve into some practical methods for conducting conversations directly with stakeholders using the PUGSIE and PUPSS frameworks. Developed over several years, these frameworks ensure communication is structured, concise, and impactful. By using these methods, you can more easily engage stakeholders and align their understanding with your UX principles.

The PUGSIE framework

PUGSIE stands for Problem, Users, Goals, Scenarios, Ideate, and Experiment. It is a simple but effective approach for capturing and communicating user experience requirements on a whiteboard. It's easy to remember and can be used as a design workshop or as a simple method for capturing a UX brief from the business during a meeting.

Write or type out the key sections below as steps to complete when engaging your team or stakeholders. Guide them through each step, ensuring you fill out each part systematically together. This approach not only helps you gather important information but also frames the conversation about the problem and user needs, while educating them on the basic principles of Lean UX.

P is for Problem

Start by helping Stakeholders to clearly define the problem that needs to be solved. This helps stakeholders properly understand the context and the importance of addressing the issue – What problems are driving this piece of work?

- *Example problem*: "We are seeing a high drop-off rate on our checkout page, which indicates users are struggling to complete their purchases."

- "We think this is due to unclear instructions, slow loading times, or a poor experience using the multi-step checkout."
- "Recent usability tests showed that 60% of users felt frustrated with the multiple steps required to enter their payment information."

U is for Users

Identify who the users are for this piece of work.

- *Example*: "We are designing for New 'non account' customers" and "Returning 'logged in' account customers."

G is for Goals

Determine what the users' goals are - what do they want to achieve? Additionally, identify the business goals - what do we want them to do? What would be a successful outcome to the goal?

- *Example user goal*: "Users want to check out items in their cart with minimum time and effort."
- *Example business goal:* "Our goal is to reduce the checkout drop-off rate"
- *Example successful outcome:* "A significant reduction in the time it takes for users to complete the checkout process, and a decrease in the checkout drop-off rate."

S is for Scenarios

Describe or sketch out a typical step-by-step scenario that helps illustrate the problem and begin to do a high-level flow or scenario map on the whiteboard.

- *Example scenario*: "A user adds an item to their cart. They click or tap on the cart icon and see the shopping cart page. They review their items and click or tap 'Checkout now' They are asked to 'Login or Continue as a Guest'... etc."

I is for Ideation

Start actioning some ideas to help solve the problem.

- Start sketching out a solution.
- Ask stakeholders to declare any ideas they have.
- Ask stakeholders to clarify their ideas by handing them the whiteboard marker or allowing them to collaborate with you directly on a digital whiteboard such as Miro.

E is for Experimentation

Tell stakeholders that you will refine the concept and iterate it through user feedback.

- Propose your next steps, such as building a prototype and conducting unmoderated user testing to gather initial feedback.

Using the PUGSIE framework helps structure your conversations on a whiteboard in a simple way that stakeholders can easily relate to. It ensures that all critical aspects are covered, allowing them to see the full picture and understand that the next logical step is to conduct user testing to validate the ideas they have helped create.

During this conversation, capture as much detail as you can, such as documenting any assumptions stakeholders may have, specific requirements, technical limitations, or writing up a hypothesis statement for your proposed experiment.

The PUPSS Framework

The PUPSS conversation framework is a streamlined version of PUGSIE, designed for quick, on-the-fly conversations. It's ideal for situations where you're suddenly asked for your UX input in a meeting, or if a conversation is going sideways and you want to bring it back to the core of what you're trying to achieve.

Remember these key points: Problem, Users, Purpose, Scenario, and Success.

Here's how you can use PUPSS effectively by asking stakeholders the following questions during your conversation:

Problem
What's the problem you're trying to solve?

Users
Who are the users we are designing for?

Purpose
What's the primary purpose of the page or feature we are designing? (Consider both user and business perspectives)

Scenario
Describe a typical scenario in which the problem occurs.

Success
What specific results would make this project successful?

The PUPSS framework is perfect for quick discussions where you need to convey essential information succinctly.

Remember, the PUGSIE and PUPSS frameworks are conversation tools designed to guide you in asking the right questions and steering the discussion in the right direction. Always delve deeper, asking plenty of probing questions and adding extra details if needed to thoroughly understand the problem and stakeholder perspectives in detail.

Practical Application of PUGSIE and PUPSS

Here are some practical tips for conducting effective conversations with stakeholders using the PUGSIE and PUPSS conversation frameworks:

- **Prepare in Advance**: Before any meeting or conversation, see if you can outline the key points you want to cover. This preparation will help you stay focused and ensure you cover all necessary aspects.

- **Be Concise:** Stick to the framework and avoid unnecessary diversions. Some stakeholders will go off on tangents, so it's important to keep the discussion focused.

- **Use a Parking Lot:** A parking lot is a designated space on the whiteboard to note down topics or questions that arise but are not immediately relevant to the current discussion. It is useful for keeping the conversation on track while ensuring important points are not forgotten. Simply say, "That's a great point. In the interest of time, let's add it to the parking lot for now and come back to it later."

- **Use Visual Aids:** Whenever possible, support your conversation with visual aids like diagrams, flowcharts, or personas. Whether it's materials you've prepared in advance or items you sketch on the fly, visuals can really help stakeholders grasp concepts quickly and effectively.

- **Listen and Adapt**: Pay attention to stakeholder feedback and be ready to adapt your approach if you have to. Use their input to refine your understanding and improve your communication style for next time.

- **Follow Up**: After any conversation, send a summary of the key points discussed and the agreed-upon next steps, if relevant. This reinforces your message and ensures everyone is on the same page.

By integrating the PUGSIE and PUPSS frameworks into your communication strategy you can more easily address UX challenges on the go, engage stakeholders, and drive more successful outcomes.

Chapter 8: Simple Techniques to Manage Difficult Conversations

As a UX or product designer, you'll frequently encounter scenarios where your work is criticised. It's easy to feel frustrated, especially when you've invested significant effort into a design solution. You might face stakeholders with preconceived notions, lack sufficient evidence to support your design decisions, or be overruled by the highest-paid person's opinion (HiPPO).

Now, let's delve into some ways of managing difficult individuals, an essential skill for any UX designer. This chapter will equip you with some simple strategies to help you handle obstructive criticism and defend your design decisions confidently and professionally, without appearing defensive.

Embracing Openness

First of all, when you feel like you've been put on the spot, remember that it's okay to admit when you don't have all the answers. Being transparent about needing time to assess a situation fosters openness and invites constructive feedback. This approach encourages discussions rather than debates.

When faced with challenging critique, try to ask questions to understand what the critic is trying to achieve. This not only buys you time but also helps you align your response with their goals. For example, asking "What are your thoughts on this?" or "What did you have in mind?" shows interest and shifts the conversation towards problem-solving, moving away from differences of opinion.

Anticipate Disagreements

One effective strategy is to anticipate potential criticisms before presenting your design. Review your work with a trusted colleague to identify weak points and prepare responses. Preempting objections during your presentation can disarm critics and demonstrate your thoroughness.

Redirect the Conversation

If a discussion becomes circular and unproductive, it's essential to recognise this and steer the conversation back on track. You can say, "This is a great discussion, but let's table it for now and revisit it later." This approach prevents wasting time on unresolved debates.

Leverage Your Design Skills

Visual aids can significantly enhance your communication. Instead of lengthy debates, use a whiteboard session to illustrate your points. Visuals help bridge the gap between different languages spoken by developers, project managers, and designers, creating a shared understanding.

Use Data to Support Your Design

Sometimes a design decision may seem obvious to you, but it's important to back even the simplest choices with some form of data or evidence. User research, analytics, and industry insights can provide compelling support for your decisions. Present this data early in the project to align everyone with your perspective.

Provide Choices

Presenting multiple design options can turn a potentially contentious discussion into a collaborative decision-making process. Offer two or three valid solutions and discuss their pros and cons. This approach transforms the conversation from defending a single design to evaluating the options together.

Get Them Excited

Identify what excites your stakeholders, whether it's data, user feedback, or visual demonstrations in a PowerPoint presentation. Use these elements to engage them and gain their support. For example, for some stakeholders, including a heatmap from a visual analytics tool like Hotjar or Mouseflow can provide powerful insights and win them over. For others, a compelling video* of a user discussing a key pain point can be particularly persuasive.

*Remember to ensure compliance with privacy regulations when sharing user videos.

Build Your Support Network through Co-Design

It's worth reiterating again the significance of collaborative design techniques, as they are crucial for building buy-in and support for your work. Embracing a co-design mentality not only improves the final product but also establishes a strong support network within your team. This collaborative approach ensures that when you face difficult stakeholders, you have a united front and collective backing for your ideas and solutions.

Having allies within your team makes defending your design decisions easier. Educate and involve team members from various departments in the UX process. When others understand and respect your work, they can help advocate for your designs, making your job smoother.

First-hand Experience

Engaging stakeholders in the UX process at every step is crucial, especially for managing difficult conversations. This can include interviewing them as Subject Matter Experts (SMEs), inviting them to observe customer interviews, and encouraging their participation in co-design workshops. By involving stakeholders in these ways, you can integrate their insights into the design process, address concerns early, and create a collaborative environment. This approach helps align everyone with the project's goals and turns potential disagreements into opportunities for productive discussions.

Learning and Practicing Conversation Frameworks

To navigate difficult conversations and keep the focus on user problems rather than debates, learn and practice the PUGSIE and PUPSS conversation frameworks, which we covered earlier in the book. The PUGSIE Framework helps structure detailed conversations during an interactive whiteboard session. The PUPSS Framework is a streamlined version for quicker, effective 'on-the-fly' discussions in meetings. These frameworks guide conversations back on track, ensuring they remain productive and user-centred.

In Summary

Dealing with difficult people is an inevitable part of any job, including UX design. By adopting the right mindset and using the tips presented, you can navigate these situations effectively. Remember, the primary goal is to create the best possible user experience, which sometimes means patiently guiding others towards it.

Chapter 9: Learning How to Back Yourself

Approaching any discussion or debate requires practice and a shift in mindset. Rather than being argumentative about your opinions, focus on being assertive and clearly articulating your point of view.

Defending design decisions is a term I encountered early in my career, where I was often asked to advocate for a particular idea or approach—usually something predetermined by personal preference, budget or feasibility. The term "defend" immediately sets a combative tone, positioning you against the stakeholder. It's important to move away from this mentality.

Here are some tips to help you gain an edge, regardless of where you are at in your career journey:

Don't Be the Sensitive Designer

It's natural to feel personally attached to your work, especially when you believe it's the right solution. However, remember that even the best designs won't always be met with open arms. Critique is part of the process, and criticism is about the design, not you.

It can be frustrating, but remember that emotions, while natural, should not drive design decisions. A strong UX and product designer learns to leave feelings behind and works to align everyone towards a common goal.

Separate Yourself from Your Design

Remember - you are not your design. It's challenging to detach yourself from your designs, but it's crucial. Multiple people or teams might resist ideas for various reasons, such as not wanting additional work for developers or managing conflicting business requirements.

Embrace the Benefits of Collaborating

UX design is rarely the responsibility of just the UX designer. Embrace a holistic view of design. It's not about you against them; it's about everyone working together for the user's benefit. A team of developers, project managers, business analysts, stakeholders, and others in your team all influence the final product. They can all contribute valuable perspectives, even if they aren't directly designing a user interface.

Overcome Your Fears of Presenting

Presenting doesn't come naturally to everyone and often requires hard work and practice. Even experienced designers can find presenting challenging, depending on the context and audience.

Presenting outside your comfort zone helps you grow. For example, when I presented my first book at its launch to a fairly large audience, I was nervous because I realised many in the audience were not familiar with UX, and there were a lot of blank faces looking back at me. After that experience, I remembered to tailor my message to my audience, enhancing my future presentations.

It helps to remember that a fear of presenting often stems from our primal survival instincts, triggering the fight or flight response. A fight or flight response can cloud our judgment and affect our ability to think clearly.

A bad presentation can exacerbate this fear, causing us to dwell on the fear rather than focus on delivering a great presentation next time. It's important to develop tools and strategies to build the confidence for presenting over time.

Drop the 'Performer' Mentality

Overcoming a fear of presenting starts with shifting your mindset from being a 'performer' to a 'communicator'. You're not aiming to deliver the best TED Talk; you're just there to convey your message as effectively as you can to your audience. Early in my career, I often compared myself to much more experienced presenters, which led to insecurity about presenting. But remember, presenting is just another form of communication.

Just focus on communicating your idea, challenge, or solution clearly. This shift will alleviate the pressure of perfection and allow you to make mistakes and learn from them. Adapt your presentations to fit your audience and continuously improve your style.

Lastly, know that it's okay to fail. It's okay to tell your audience, "I'm still learning and growing." This honesty not only humanises you but also allows you to keep improving.

Rehearse and Refine

To overcome presentation anxiety, change your mindset by practicing repeatedly until presenting becomes a habit. Like my friend who became a confident presenter after working at a top New York agency and presenting almost every day, consistent practice can build confidence.

Practice your presentation, even if it's just on your own. Even better - find a trusted colleague to review it with you, helping to iron out mistakes and receive feedback. For crucial presentations, record yourself to identify and adjust any quirks in your style.

Visualise Success

Visualisation is a technique used by athletes to boost confidence. Run through your presentation in your mind, imagining a calm and confident delivery. Knowing the setting and audience size can help make your visualisation more accurate. This technique can be practiced anywhere - on the bus, out for a walk, even at home whilst laying in bed.

Project Confidence

Even if you don't feel confident, act as if you are. Body language and tone of voice play a crucial role in communication. According to experts, only 7% of communication is verbal, while 93% is non-verbal (body language and tone). Practice projecting confidence through your body language and tone to influence your audience positively.

Mastering Body Language

Confident body language can make you feel more assured. Here are some key tips:

- **Keep Your Chin Up:** Maintaining an upright posture signals confidence.

- **Uncross Your Arms:** Open posture promotes a more receptive attitude.

- **Face Your Audience:** Direct your body squarely at your audience to show engagement.

- **Avoid Fidgeting:** Stay still to exude strength and confidence. Use hand gestures only to emphasise points.

- **Choose Words and Tone Carefully:** Choose positive words to set a positive mood.

- **Be Open:** Maintain an open posture to encourage an open attitude.

Putting Others at Ease

Your body language and tone can also help put others at ease.

These tips also work well in smaller presentations:

- **Encourage Openness:** Use activities that involve physical movement, such as workshop activities. These can help break down barriers.
- **Mirror Your Audience:** Align your body language with others in the room to create a connection.
- **Smile:** A smile can ease tension and make the audience more receptive.

While it's OK to portray an informal or light-hearted approach to presenting, it's best to avoid cracking jokes in presentations. At least until you've reached a pro-skill level!

Developing the right mindset for presenting involves continuous practice. Remember, presenting is about communication, not performance. Stay open, adaptable, and project confidence, and you will find your presentations becoming increasingly successful.

Chapter 10: The Art of Presenting

Some people seem to be natural presenters and can easily stand up in front of a room full of strangers with a TED talk swagger. If you're one of those people, then good for you! But for the vast majority, it doesn't come naturally and takes both hard work and practice before it becomes easier.

I remember at university, we all had to stand up in front of about 100 people and present a piece of design work for the first time. Most people were extremely nervous. Some of my colleagues were natural presenters and did an amazing job, but many others stuttered, mumbled, and went bright red. One person ran out of the room, and at least two people were conveniently off sick that day.

For me, the best way to approach presenting is to be thoroughly prepared: knowing my content inside out and being clear on the narrative—what story are we telling? This is a common theme among all good presenters: having an engaging narrative.

This chapter will guide you to confident presentations by helping you structure your presentations in the right way. These techniques will help you engage and persuade your audience, ensuring your UX insights resonate and make a significant impact.

Preparing for a Design Presentation

- **Know Your Outcomes:** Be clear about what you want to achieve.
- **Understand Your Audience:** Tailor your story to align with business goals and use appropriate business language.

- **Dry-run:** Conduct a dry-run with a colleague to check for errors and ensure clarity.

Conducting a Design Presentation

- **Set the scene:** Start with a clear and concise overview, then delve into details.
- **Define the Purpose:** Clearly articulate the problem, outcomes, and process.
- **Stay focused:** Keep the focus on the problem and business goals.
- **Be Open to Feedback:** Recognise valid input and explore underlying needs.
- **Confirm Understanding:** Actively confirm by summarising and repeating what people have said.
- **Manage Your Tone:** Stay curious and interested, even when receiving critique.

After the Design Presentation

- **Collate Your Notes:** Collect and consider all feedback before deciding on actions.
- **Follow Up:** Confirm what was discussed and clarify any confusion.
- **Address Individuals Directly:** Consider having direct conversations with those who provided feedback.

Presentation Methods

As a UX or product designer, you'll often need to present your work to various audiences. Understanding how to tailor your presentation to different types of listeners is key to your success. Let's explore two methods to do this: deductive and inductive.

Deductive Presentations - Logical and Direct

The deductive method is straightforward and works well for technical or analytical audiences who appreciate a simple and sequential flow. If you've conducted a presentation before, it's likely you've followed this format, as it's a logical and direct way to present information.

There are a few ways to format a deductive presentation, but here's a common approach:

1. **Start with a Key Insight:** Begin by presenting your main point.

2. **Support it with Evidence:** Provide multiple insights or evidence that back up your point.

If it's based on user feedback, you're likely to include sections that explain the problem, the design you tested, the participants, what you discovered, the data to support it, and your design recommendations, concluding with suggested next steps, such as further testing or moving to detailed designs.

While this method is clear and logical, it can sometimes lead to lengthy presentations with lots of slides and may not appeal to time-poor stakeholders who just want quick answers or those who get distracted easily.

Inductive Presentations - Engaging and Story-Driven

The inductive method is perfect for engaging busy stakeholders and executives. It's about storytelling and allowing your audience to draw their own conclusions from the narrative you present.

Structuring an Inductive Presentation

1. **Master Vision or Theme:** Start with a compelling vision or theme. Think of it like a movie trailer that sets the stage and captures attention.

2. **Current State:** Describe the current situation or problem, including high-level metrics or background information.

3. **Problem to Solve:** Clearly articulate the problem and key issues, relating them back to your main theme.

4. **Desired Future State:** Paint a picture of the future where the problem is solved. Explain the benefits of your solution.

5. **Call to Action:** Ask for their input on your design ideas. Propose several options to steer the discussion towards making a choice.

6. **Appendix: The Evidence:** Provide detailed statistics and evidence for those interested in delving deeper.

Example: A Seamless Shopping Experience

Master Vision or Theme:

"We propose creating a shopping experience where every step feels intuitive and effortless. Our goal is to transform our current e-commerce platform into this seamless shopping experience, delighting our users and driving higher conversion rates."

Current State:

"Currently, our checkout process has a high drop-off rate, with 40% of users abandoning their carts at the payment stage. Feedback indicates that users find the process cumbersome and confusing."

Problem to Solve:

"The key issue is the complexity of our multi-step checkout process, which frustrates users and leads to cart abandonment. Users expect a quicker and more straightforward experience."

Desired Future State:

"Our vision is a single-step checkout process that is mobile-first, clear, and efficient. This streamlined process will reduce friction, increase user satisfaction, and decrease the drop-off rate by 20%."

Call to Action:

"We need your input on the proposed design solutions. Should we prioritise implementing the single-step checkout, or focus first on optimising the current multi-step process? Your feedback will help us decide the best course of action."

Appendix: The Evidence:

"Detailed user feedback, heatmaps showing where users drop off, and statistics from our usability tests will be available for those interested in a deeper dive into the data supporting this initiative."

When to Choose Inductive over Deductive

The inductive method, which emphasises storytelling, often resonates better with an executive audience. It's less about proving your point with data upfront and more about engaging your listeners with a narrative they can connect to.

The Power of Storytelling

Good storytelling can make your presentation memorable and impactful (but it doesn't need to be a TED talk either).

Here's why it's essential:

- **Engagement:** Stories capture attention and make complex information relatable.
- **Empathy:** They help your audience understand and empathise with user experiences.
- **Inspiration:** A well-told story can inspire action and support for your ideas.

Creating Your Elevator Pitch

Capture your vision in a short, succinct statement. Clearly articulate the value your work delivers, especially for executives. This helps set the tone for your presentation and engages your audience from the start.

Shaping Your Story

Start by capturing your audience's imagination. Use a structure that highlights the current state versus the desired future state. This approach makes the future more appealing and draws your audience into a better world for the customer.

Using Video to Tell a Story

Consider using video to make your presentation even more engaging. A video can bring your story to life and make it more dynamic than a traditional slide deck.

Showing Your Evidence

After telling your story, present your detailed evidence. Think of this as the credits in a movie, where those interested can delve deeper into the details of your design process.

In Summary

Mastering the art of presenting involves understanding your audience and choosing the right method. By using the inductive method, you can make your presentations more engaging, persuasive, and memorable. Storytelling is at the heart of an inductive format, and this is your ally in selling your vision and creating a more compelling presentation to stakeholders.

Chapter 11: Nine Simple Steps to Kickstart Your Success

You've journeyed through the essentials of communicating UX design to others, from adopting the right mindset to mastering difficult conversations and presentation skills. This final chapter provides practical steps to continue your journey. These "kick-start" steps are designed to help you start small and build up, setting you on the path to success in a straightforward and manageable way.

Keep these steps handy and work through them as needed. You can pick and choose which actions to do first, in any order, based on your comfort level, but don't be tempted to skip them completely. Making the effort with each one will elevate you into a better and more effective communicator with your stakeholders and co-workers.

Step 1: Find a Mentor

Whether you are just starting out or have been on your journey for a while, it's important to recognise where you are and where you need to grow. Always show an eagerness to learn and leverage the expertise of those willing to share their knowledge and help you. Remember, no one person could ever know everything there is to know about UX and product design. And anyone who says or acts like they do has simply stopped looking for more.

Kick-Start Actions:

- Find a mentor

Step 2: Understand Your Audience

Tailoring your communication style to resonate with your audience ensures your messages are clear and relatable. This approach fosters better collaboration and support for your UX initiatives.

Kick-Start Actions:

- Create team personas.
- Conduct stakeholder interviews or discussions.

Step 3: Learn Conversation Frameworks

Understanding the T.E.S.L.A. principles and practicing conversation frameworks such as PUGSIE and PUPSS, can help you become more effective talking about your UX process and running ad-hoc design sessions more comfortably.

Kick-start Actions:

- Learn and practice the PUPSS conversation framework.
- Build up to more involved stakeholder workshops and whiteboard sessions using the PUGSIE framework.
- Rehearse and refine these communication techniques regularly.

Step 4: Back Your Designs with Evidence

While it may seem obvious, compelling UX research provides the evidence needed to support your design decisions. It also helps educate your colleagues about user needs and behaviours, ensuring that the business makes informed decisions that align with user goals. Remember, you can always do something, whether it's analysing site data, collating user comments, or showcasing industry case studies.

Kick-start Actions:

- Conduct user research with real users.
- If formal user testing isn't possible, try guerrilla or corridor testing.
- Conduct a landscape or industry review (desk research).
- Showcase industry case studies.
- Bring user comments and success data to meetings.

Step 5: Master the Art of Co-Design

Aligning UX design with business goals ensures that your design efforts contribute to the overall success of the organisation. Co-design workshops help align team members and stakeholders around user needs, fostering a shared understanding and commitment to UX principles.

Kick-start Actions:

- Regularly conduct co-design workshops.
- Start small with design sessions on a whiteboard.
- Create user proto-personas with your team.
- Work towards more strategic workshops to establish a shared UX vision, such as a UX principles workshop.

Step 6: Use Inductive 'Story-telling' Presentations

Practicing presentation methods, including the inductive approach, is crucial for engaging stakeholders, decision-makers, and executives. By using a story-telling format, you can create a more compelling narrative that captures your audience's attention and effectively conveys your UX vision and encourages buy-in.

Kick-start Actions:

- Know who you are talking to and tailor your presentations accordingly.
- Connect your UX vision with business goals using the inductive presentation method.
- Rehearse important presentations and refine them early with the help of a peer.
- Practice open and confident body language to help reinforce your messages.
- Incorporate feedback to learn and grow, continually improving your presentation skills.

Step 7: Adopt the Influencer Mindset

Transitioning from a design implementer to a design influencer empowers you to guide your team and organisation. Empathising with both users and stakeholders builds trust and encourages collaboration.

Kick-start Actions:

- Involve co-workers and stakeholders in user testing sessions.

- Attend speaking events and share your learnings.
- Showcase interesting case studies you find.
- Collaborate with other departments to align UX goals with broader business objectives.
- Join or form a design community.
- Become a mentor - Pass on learnings to junior team members to foster a culture of continuous learning and improvement.

Step 8: Become a UX Evangelist

By being the leader who shares user insights and success stories, you can help dispel misconceptions, highlight the impact of UX, and inspire others to support and engage with your design practices. Actively selling the value of proper user experience design methods in your organisation is crucial, whether it's through well-placed slides in a design presentation or dedicated UX roadshows to sell the whole vision.

Kick-start Actions:

- Continually reiterate the UX process and its benefits in your design presentations.
- Create regular updates or newsletters highlighting your teams UX achievements.
- Conduct a "What is UX" roadshow.
- Conduct workshops on a UX vision or UX principles to onboard others with the value of UX.
- Evangelise your UX vision and principles to stakeholders through presentations or informal discussions.
- Create a UX dashboard to track and showcase success metrics.

Step 9: Develop a UX Growth Mindset

A growth mindset is vital for any UX designer. Try to see mistakes as opportunities to learn and improve. Remember, each organisation is unique, so be ready to adapt based on feedback. Think of your UX practice as a design experiment–constantly iterate, refine, and evolve your approach.

As a UX professional, owning your shortcomings and being transparent about your knowledge and limitations is respectable and fosters trust.

Kick-start Actions:

- Stay curious and keep learning.
- Have empathy for your users and colleagues.
- Be confident in your abilities.
- Embrace feedback and use it to grow.

Chapter 12: Final Word

You've now completed this journey of communicating UX within your organisation. This guide has presented you with some simple tools and advice to develop the right mindset, conduct conversations clearly, and present your ideas effectively. By following these practical steps, my hope is that you can continue to grow as a UX or product designer, more easily navigating common communication challenges, and foster a culture that truly values the user in user experience.

This quick guide was designed to help you digest important information quickly, and I hope it helps elevate your career to more success.

Good luck on your UX journey, and may you continue to make the world a better place for your users and the business you work for.

Thank you so much for reading.

www.ingramcontent.com/pod-product-compliance
Lightning Source LLC
Chambersburg PA
CBHW071951210526
45479CB00003B/895